Wonders

Reading/Writing Companion

Mc
Graw
Hill

mheducation.com/prek-12

Send all inquiries to:
McGraw Hill
1325 Avenue of the Americas
New York, NY 10019

ISBN: 978-1-26-573078-9
MHID: 1-26-573078-4

Printed in the United States of America.

3 4 5 6 7 8 9 LMN 26 25 24 23 22

A

Welcome to WONDERS!

We are so excited about how much you will learn and grow this year! We're here to help you set goals for your learning.

You will build on what you already know and learn new things every day.

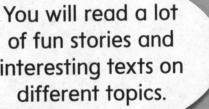

You will read a lot of fun stories and interesting texts on different topics.

You will write about the texts you read. You will also write texts of your own. You will do research as well.

You will explore new ideas by reading different texts.

Each week, we will set goals on the My Goals page. Here is an example:

I can read and understand realistic fiction.

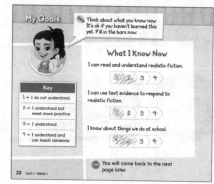

I've never read realistic fiction. I'll shade the **first box**.

I want some more practice with realistic fiction, so I'll shade the first **two boxes**.

I can read and understand realistic fiction. I'll shade in **three boxes**.

I've read a lot of realistic fiction and I like to share what I know. I'll shade all **four boxes**.

As you read and write, you will learn skills and strategies to help you reach your goals.

You will think about your learning and sometimes fill in a bar to show your progress.

| Check In | 1 | 2 | 3 | 4 |

Here are some questions you can ask yourself.

- Did I understand the task?
- Was it easy?
- Was it hard?
- What made it hard?

It is okay if I need more practice. The most important thing is to do my best and keep learning!

If you need more support, you can choose what to do.

- Talk to a friend or teacher.
- Use an Anchor Chart.
- Choose a center activity.

At the end of each week, you will complete a fun task to show what you have learned.

Then you will return to your My Goals page and think about your learning.

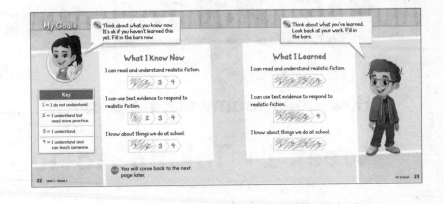

Unit 6 Together We Can!

The Big Idea

Week 1 • Taking Action

Digital Tools *Find this eBook and other resources at:* my.mheducation.com

Week 2 • My Team

SOCIAL STUDIES

LWA/The Image Bank/Getty Images

Week 3 • Weather Together

Week 4 • Sharing Traditions

Week 5 • Celebrate America!

Extended Writing

Opinion Text

Connect and Reflect

SOCIAL STUDIES

Image Source/Getty Images

Unit 6

Together We Can!

Listen to and think about the poem, "Together."

 Talk about the children in the photo. How are they better together?

The
Big Idea

How does teamwork help us?

Build Knowledge

Essential Question How can we work together to make our lives better?

Build Vocabulary

 Talk with your partner about ways people can work together to make our lives better.

 Write words about working together.

paint a mural in a park

Working Together

My Goals

 Think about what you know now. What do you want to work on more? Fill in the bars.

What I Know Now

I can read and understand a fantasy story.

| 1 | 2 | 3 | 4 |

I can respond to a fantasy story by writing a new story.

| 1 | 2 | 3 | 4 |

I know about ways we can work together to make our lives better.

| 1 | 2 | 3 | 4 |

Key

1 = I do not understand.

2 = I understand but need more practice.

3 = I understand.

4 = I understand and can teach someone.

 You will come back to the next page later.

What I Learned

I can read and understand a fantasy story.

1 > 2 > 3 > 4 >

I can respond to a fantasy story by writing a new story.

1 > 2 > 3 > 4 >

I know about ways we can work together to make our lives better.

1 > 2 > 3 > 4 >

My Goal I can read and understand a fantasy story.

Find Text Evidence

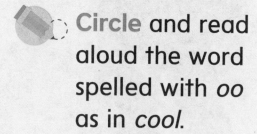 **Read** to find out how a group of tools works together.

Circle and read aloud the word spelled with *oo* as in *cool*.

Essential Question

? How can we work together to make our lives better?

Super Tools

🔍 **Find Text Evidence**

Underline and read aloud the word *brought*.

Ask questions if something in the story doesn't make sense. Then reread to see if it makes sense now.

A few weeks ago, Lucy's mom and dad brought a new computer home. "This is so cool!" exclaimed Lucy. Lucy used the computer all the time.

But not everyone was happy about the new computer.

Lucy didn't know it, but her writing tools felt sad and useless. One day while she was at school, they had an **emergency** meeting.

"Lucy hasn't used us in weeks!" cried the markers. "Can we **demand** to be used?" asked the crayons. "No, that would be rude. But, we can remind her how great we are," said the pencils. "Yes!" they all agreed. "Let's remind her."

Find Text Evidence

Think about what you read. Reread and look at the pictures if you don't understand something.

Underline and read aloud the words *door*, *busy*, and *enough*.

After school, as soon as Lucy came through the door, she grabbed a glass of juice and went right to her computer. She had to write a report about birds.

The writing tools watched and waited. When Lucy was done, she printed her report.

That night the writing tools got busy. They worked together to make a picture for Lucy.

The pencils made a sketch. The markers drew the birds in the tree. The crayons drew the Sun in a blue sky. The picture was good enough to frame.

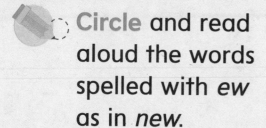 **Find Text Evidence**

Circle and read aloud the words spelled with *ew* as in *new*.

Talk about why Lucy wishes she had drawn the picture.

The next day was Saturday. Lucy woke up late. Then she went to get her report. Lucy gasped. She couldn't believe her eyes! "Who drew this great picture?" she asked.

"Did you draw this?" Lucy asked Mom and Dad. "You know the answer to that!" they laughed. "Stop joking! YOU drew that great picture."

That made Lucy think she wished she had drawn it. "It is fun to draw," she said.

Find Text Evidence

Retell the story using the illustrations and words to help you.

Lucy hung the picture in her room. Then she took out her pencils, crayons, and markers. "I'll draw my own picture for my report," she said.

Lucy and her pencils, crayons, and markers worked together. They drew a super picture.

From that day on, Lucy kept drawing. And the writing tools felt happy and useful!

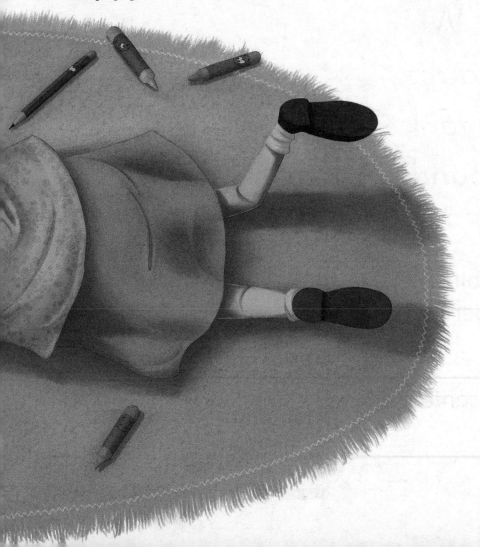

Writing Practice

Write a Paragraph

 Talk about how Lucy likes to draw.

 Listen to this paragraph about a hobby.

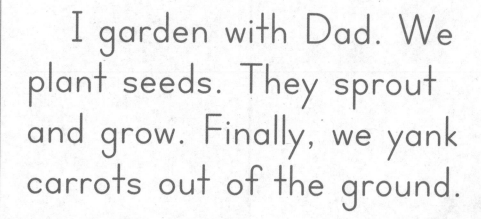

I garden with Dad. We plant seeds. They sprout and grow. Finally, we yank carrots out of the ground.

Underline the opening sentence blue. Underline the details orange. Underline the concluding statement green.

Circle the strong verb in the last sentence.

Talk about your favorite hobby.

Write a paragraph about your favorite hobby. Include an opening sentence, details, a concluding statement, and strong verbs. Make sure you indent the first line.

_____

- -

_____

_____

- -

_____

_____

- -

_____

Underline the opening sentence blue. Underline the details orange. Underline the concluding statement green. You can use your finger to make sure you indent.

Circle the strong verbs you used.

Check In | 1 | 2 | 3 | 4

Vocabulary

 Listen to the sentences and look at the photos.

 Talk about the words.

 Write your own sentence using each word.

demand

People can **demand** fair pay.

_____

- -

_____

emergency

A fire is one kind of **emergency**.

_____

- -

_____

A synonym is a word that has almost the same meaning as another word.

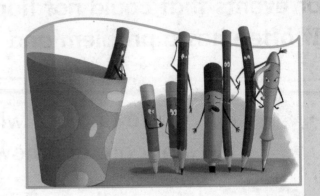

Find Text Evidence

I read the word *exclaimed* in the story. *Exclaimed* and *said* are synonyms. They both mean that someone "spoke words."

"This is so cool!" exclaimed Lucy.

Your Turn

What is a synonym for the word *happy* on page 16? Use a dictionary or thesaurus if you need help.

_____

- - - - - - - - - - - - - - - - - - -

_____

_____

| Check In | 1 | 2 | 3 | 4 |

A **fantasy** story has made-up characters or events that could not happen in real life. It often has a problem and solution.

 Reread to find out what the problems in the story are and how they are solved.

 Talk about the problems and solutions.

 Write two problems and their solutions from the story.

Check In 1 2 3 4

What is the problem?	What is the solution?

The **theme** of a story is the big idea or message that an author wants to share.

 Reread "Super Tools."

 Talk about the clues in the story that help you understand the author's message.

 Write about the clues and the theme of the story.

Check In 1 2 3 4

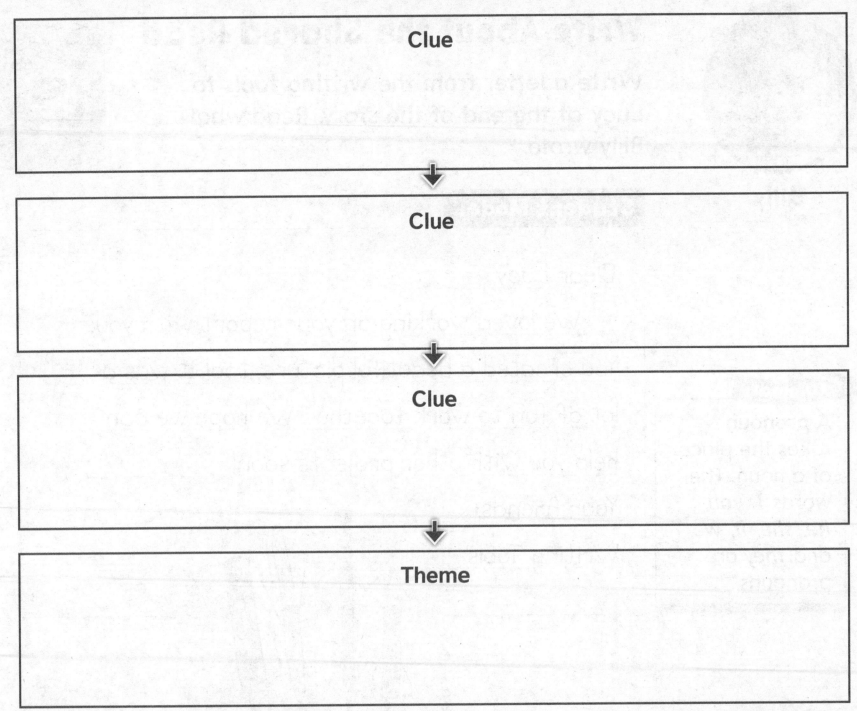

Clue

Clue

Clue

Theme

Billy

Write About the Shared Read

Write a letter from the writing tools to Lucy at the end of the story. Read what Billy wrote.

Student Model

Dear Lucy,

    We loved working on your report with you. You created a beautiful picture, too! It was a lot of fun to work together. We hope we can help you with other projects soon!

Your friends,

Writing Tools

Grammar

A **pronoun** takes the place of a noun. The words *I, you, he, she, it, we,* and *they* are pronouns.

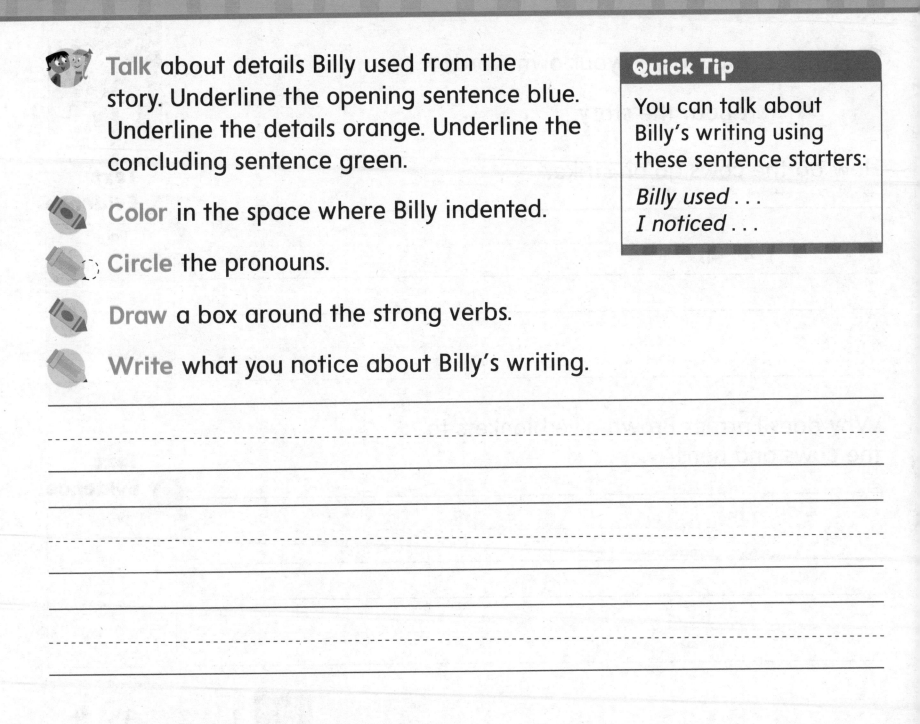

Talk about details Billy used from the story. Underline the opening sentence blue. Underline the details orange. Underline the concluding sentence green.

Color in the space where Billy indented.

Circle the pronouns.

Draw a box around the strong verbs.

Write what you notice about Billy's writing.

Quick Tip

You can talk about Billy's writing using these sentence starters:

Billy used . . .
I noticed . . .

 Retell the story in your own words.

Write about the story.

How do the cows go on strike?

Text Evidence

Page

_____

- - - - - - - - - - - - - - - - - - - -

_____

- - - - - - - - - - - - - - - - - - - -

_____

Why does Farmer Brown give blankets to
the cows and hens?

Text Evidence

Page

_____

- - - - - - - - - - - - - - - - - - - -

_____

- - - - - - - - - - - - - - - - - - - -

_____

Check In 1 2 3 4

Talk about what happens on pages 272–274.

 Write clues from the illustrations and text that show how Farmer Brown is feeling.

Text	Illustrations

How does the author show that Farmer Brown is frustrated? Share your answer.

_____

_____

_____

_____

Anchor Text

Click, Clack, Moo
Cows That Type
by Doreen Cronin
Illustrated by Betsy Lewin

Talk about what happens in the illustrations on pages 280–283.

Write clues from the text and illustrations that tell what makes Farmer Brown furious.

Clue	Clue

How does the author show that Farmer Brown is furious? Share your answer.

_____

_____

_____

_____

Talk about what happens on page 292.
What is Farmer Brown waiting for?

 Write the words that repeat in the story.

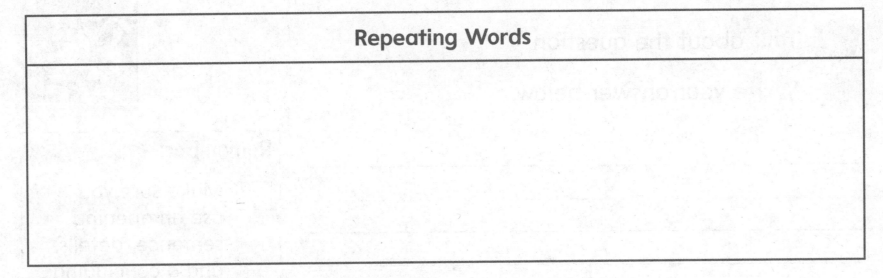

Repeating Words

What do the repeating words show?
Share your answer.

Writing and Grammar

Write About the Anchor Text

Imagine the farmer wouldn't give the ducks a diving board. Write a letter that he might receive from the animals after he says no.

 Talk about the question.

 Write your answer below.

Remember:

☐ Make sure you use an opening sentence, details, and a concluding statement. Make sure you indent.

☐ Use strong verbs in your writing.

☐ Use pronouns correctly.

Check In 1 2 3 4

Be a Volunteer!

Volunteering is an important way to help others! Volunteers can help people and animals. They can help our planet. There are many ways to volunteer.

These volunteers work at a food drive.

Read to find out about people who help others.

Underline the words that tell what volunteers do.

Talk about the author's opinion about volunteering.

Blend Images/Image Source

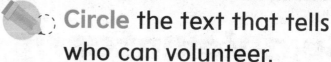

Let's read how volunteers can clean up a lake! Volunteers can plant flowers and bushes. They can also collect plastic bottles and cans to recycle. Volunteers can help remove items that don't belong in the water.

 Circle the text that tells who can volunteer.

Talk about the photo. What does this tell you about volunteering?

People of all ages can be volunteers.

Hero Images/Getty Images

Quick Tip

Look for clues in the text, photos, and captions.

Talk about what the text says about how volunteers can clean up a lake.

Write about the ways they can help.

What is the author's opinion about volunteering?

_____

- - - - - - - - - - - - - - - - -

_____

- - - - - - - - - - - - - - - - -

_____

Write About It

Write your opinion about a topic. Include a reason for your opinion.

Check In 1 > 2 > 3 > 4 >

Integrate **Research and Inquiry**

Poll About Taking Action

Step 1 **Pick** a place in school that you and your classmates can work together to improve.

Step 2 **List** three ways to be good citizens and help improve your school.

Ways to help	Number of classmates
1.	
2.	
3.	

Step 3 **Poll** your classmates about the best way to improve your school. Tally the votes for each way.

Step 4 **Write** about the results of your poll.

_____

- -

_____

- -

_____

- -

_____

- -

_____

- -

_____

Step 5 **Choose** how to present your work.

Check In   1 2 3 4

Talk about what the children in the photo are doing.

 Compare the way these children are working to the tools in "Super Tools."

People can help by keeping parks clean.

Quick Tip

You can compare the children and the writing tools using these sentence starters:

These children are . . .

The writing tools also . . .

Check In 1 2 3 4

Show Your Knowledge

My Goal I know about ways we can work together to make our lives better.

Make a Community Poster

1 **Look** at your Build Knowledge pages in your reader's notebook. What did you learn about ways we can work together?

2 **Create** a poster showing a way to help in your community. Write why people should help out. Write about how your idea is similar to or different from the ways people worked together in the texts you read. Use two vocabulary words from the Word Bank.

3 **Draw** a picture to go with your poster.

Think about what you learned this week. Fill in the bars on page 13.

Build Knowledge

Build Vocabulary

 Talk with your partner about different types of helpers.

Write words about helpers.

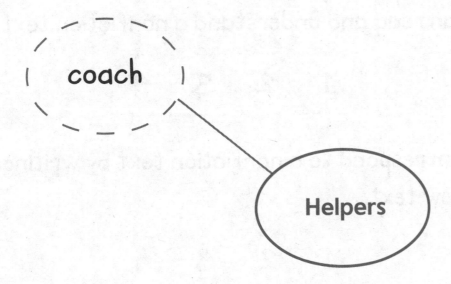

coach

Helpers

My Goals

 Think about what you know now.
This may take time and effort!
Fill in the bars.

What I Know Now

I can read and understand a nonfiction text.

| 1 | 2 | 3 | 4 |

I can respond to a nonfiction text by writing a new text.

| 1 | 2 | 3 | 4 |

I know about different people who help others.

| 1 | 2 | 3 | 4 |

Key
1 = I do not understand.
2 = I understand but need more practice.
3 = I understand.
4 = I understand and can teach someone.

 You will come back to the next page later.

Think about what you've learned.
What did you make progress with?
Fill in the bars.

What I Learned

I can read and understand a nonfiction text.

1 2 3 4

I can respond to a nonfiction text by writing a new text.

1 2 3 4

I know about different people who help others.

1 2 3 4

Shared Read

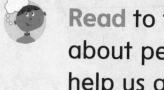

My Goal

I can read and understand a nonfiction text.

🔍 **Find Text Evidence**

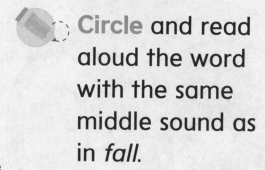

Read to find out about people who help us and how they help.

Circle and read aloud the word with the same middle sound as in *fall*.

Essential Question

? Who helps you?

Superstudio/Stone/Getty Images

All Kinds of Helpers

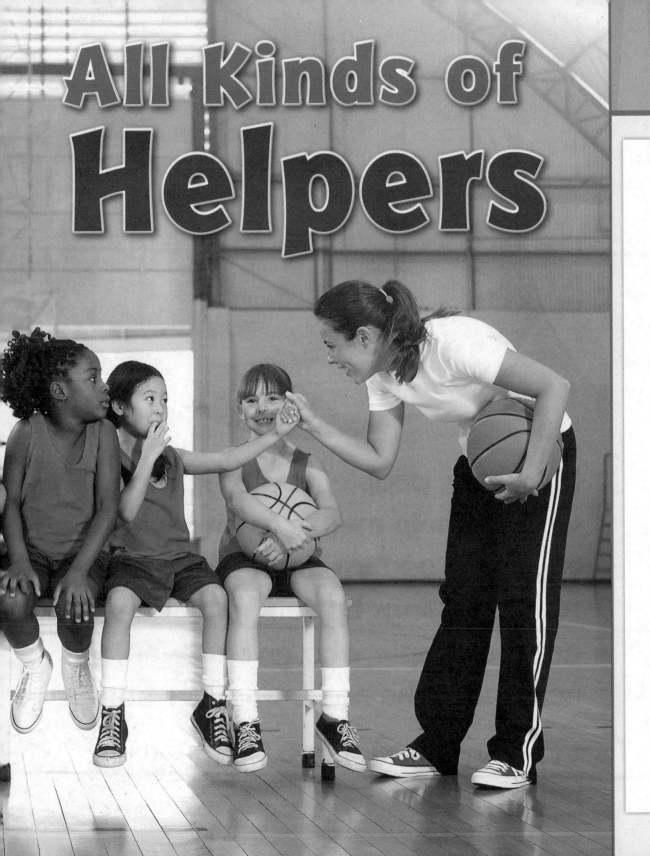

Underline the words *love*, *mother*, *father*, and *brother*.

Think about what you read. Reread and look at the photos if you do not understand something.

Every day, people help us in many ways. To help means to give what is needed and useful. It also means to make things better. So helpers are the people who give us what we need and who make our lives better.

Who are some of the people who help us?

Families can be helpers. The people in a family love and **accept** us. They also help us in many ways.

A family can include a mother and a father. This boy also has a big brother. His brother **often** helps him with his homework. His mother and father help him learn about the world.

Nonfiction

Corbis/age fotostock

Shared Read

 Find Text Evidence

 **Talk** about the people you've read about so far. Who helps you at school?

Circle and read aloud the word spelled with *augh* as in *caught*.

Teachers help you in many ways. In school, a teacher helps you learn how to read and write. A teacher teaches you subjects such as math and social studies. A teacher helps you understand new ideas.

Sports coaches are helpers, too. The baseball coach in this picture is teaching his team how to hold the ball. He talks to them and shows them what to do. Who taught you how to play a sport?

Think about what you read. Reread and look at the photos if you do not understand something.

Circle and read aloud the words spelled with *au* as in *pause* and *augh* as in *taught*.

Doctors and nurses help keep you healthy. You visit the doctor for a checkup or when you feel sick.

The girl in this picture feels awful because she caught a bad cold! But the doctor will help her get better.

Do you walk or take a bus to school? Either way, people help you get back and forth safely.

Other helpers keep you safe, too. Police officers and firefighters are always protecting you.

Find Text Evidence

 **Retell** the text so it makes sense.

Some boys and girls need a grownup to talk to. Some groups match boys and girls with a grownup who will be their friend. What a good idea!

A special group called **Big Brothers Big Sisters** helps some children out.

There are many helpers around you. Families love you, and teachers help you learn. Doctors, nurses, and safety helpers keep you healthy and safe. Special groups help you in special ways. All of them give what is needed and useful.

Nonfiction

Write a Paragraph

 Talk about the helpers from the text.

 Listen to this paragraph about a helper.

> Every day, the crossing guard helps me. She makes cars stop. She helps me cross the street safely. She is a very important helper!

 Underline the words that tell you how the writer feels.

 Circle the topic sentence.

Writing Traits

- **Using your voice** means telling how you feel and writing so it sounds like you.

- Remember, **introduce your topic.**

Talk about someone who has helped you.

 Write a paragraph about someone who has helped you. Use words that tell how you feel. Include a topic sentence.

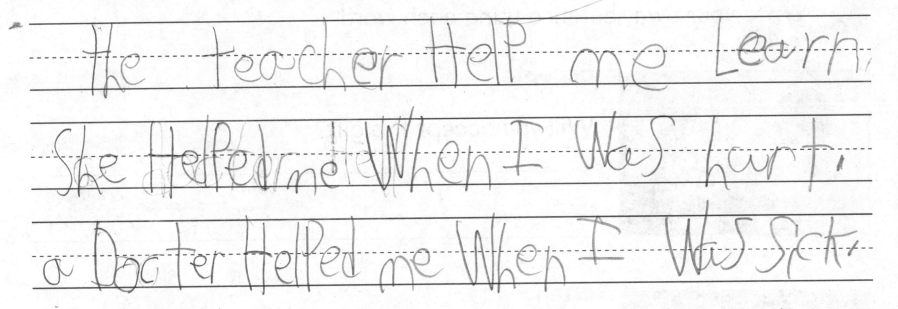

The teacher HelP me Learn.
She HelPed me When I Was hurt.
a DocTer HelPed me When I Was Sick.

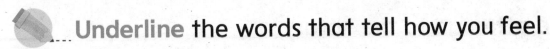 **Underline** the words that tell how you feel.

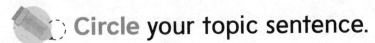 **Circle** your topic sentence.

Vocabulary

 Listen to the sentences and look at the photos.

 Talk about the words.

 Write your own sentence using each word.

accept

Will you **accept** this gift?

_____

- - - - - - - - - - - - - - - - - -

_____

often

We **often** go to the library.

_____

- - - - - - - - - - - - - - - - - -

_____

Antonyms are words with opposite meanings.

Find Text Evidence

I read the word *awful* in the text. When I look it up, I see that its antonym is *wonderful*. This helps me understand just how terrible the girl feels.

> The girl in this picture feels (awful) because she caught a bad cold!

Your Turn

What is an antonym for the word *healthy* on page 56? Use a dictionary or thesaurus if you need help.

_____

- - - - - - - - - - - - - - - - - -

_____

- - - - - - - - - - - - - - - - - -

_____

- - - - - - - - - - - - - - - - - -

_____

Check In 1 > 2 > 3 > 4

A **nonfiction** text gives facts and information about real people and things. The author may include descriptive words.

 Reread "All Kinds of Helpers."

 Talk about descriptive words on page 54.

Write about descriptive words the author uses on pages 56 and 57.

Check In 1 2 3 4

Word	What It Describes

The author's purpose is the reason why an author writes a text. The author can use information in the text and photos to explain his or her purpose.

 Reread "All Kinds of Helpers."

 Talk about the information you learn from the text and photos.

 Write the information you learn from the text and the photos. What does this information tell you about the author's purpose? Write the author's purpose.

Check In 1 2 3 4

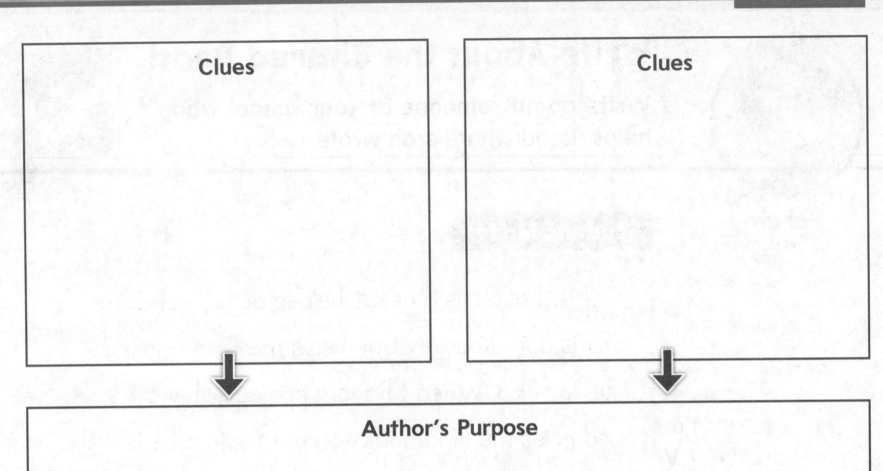

Clues

Clues

Author's Purpose

Farah

Write About the Shared Read

All Kinds of Helpers

Write about someone at your school who helps. Read what Farah wrote.

Student Model

Ms. Potter is a great helper at my school. She is our librarian. She helps me find books I like to read. When I have a project, she also helps me find books on my topic. She is very helpful!

Grammar

Possessive pronouns tell who or what has something.

Talk about details Farah used. Underline words that show Farah's feelings.

 Circle a possessive pronoun.

 Draw a box around the topic sentence.

 Write what you notice about Farah's writing.

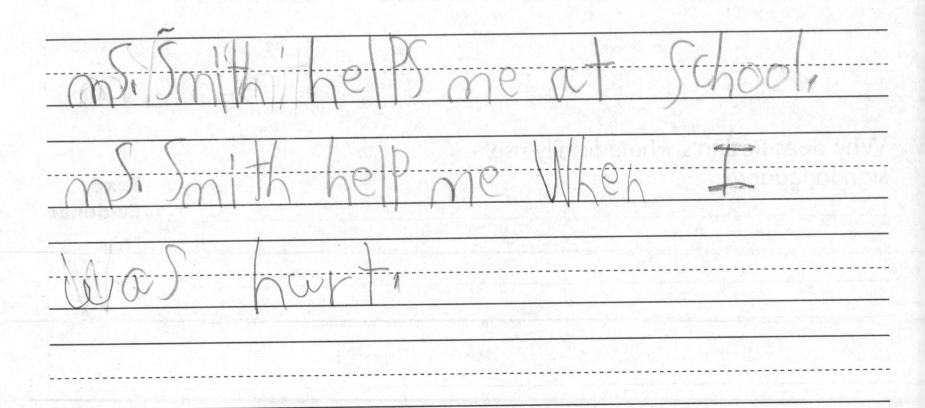

ms. Smith helps me at school.

ms. Smith help me when I

was hurt.

 Retell the text using the photos and words from the text.

Write about the text.

How do the teachers at Rosina's school teach?

_____

- -

_____

_____

- -

_____

Text Evidence

Page

Why does Rosina's whole family use sign language?

_____

- -

_____

_____

- -

_____

Text Evidence

Page

Check In | 1 > 2 > 3 > 4 >

Talk about the photo and text feature on page 304.

Write clues from the feature that help you understand how Rosina communicates.

What Text Says	What Photos Show

Why does the author include the feature at the beginning of the text? Share your answer.

_____

- -

_____

- -

_____

 Talk about what Rosina and her family are doing on pages 316–319.

Write clues from the text that tell when and where Rosina is with her family.

> **Rosina is with her family . . . .**

How does the author show that this part of the text is about Rosina's home life? Share your ideas.

_____

- -

_____

- -

_____

Talk about the photo on page 320.

 Write about who is in the photo and what they all do.

Who Are They?	What Do They Do?

What do the photo and text tell you about what's important to Rosina? Share your answer.

_____

- -

_____

- -

_____

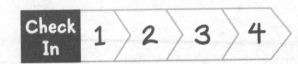

Writing and Grammar

Write About the Anchor Text

Rosina has a special community that works together. How do the people in your community work together to help you?

 Talk about the question.

 Write your answer below.

_____

- -

_____

- -

_____

Remember:

☐ Use words that tell your feelings.

☐ Include a topic sentence.

☐ Use possessive pronouns correctly.

_____

Check In 1 ⟩ 2 ⟩ 3 ⟩ 4

Paired Selection

Talk about words that repeat in each stanza.

Write the repeating words. Then write what the poet talks about doing in that place.

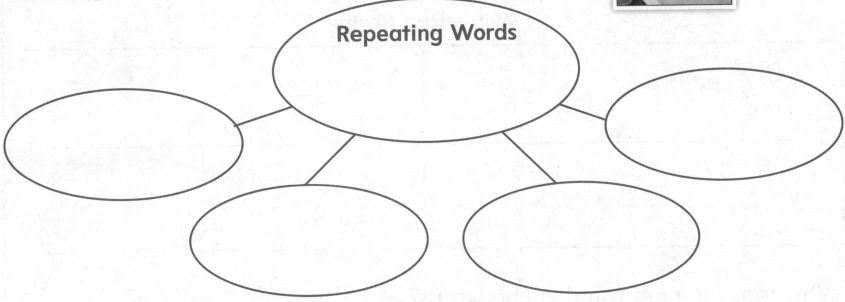

Repeating Words

Why does the poet repeat words in the poem?

_____

- -

_____

_____

- -

Quick Tip

Think about the examples the poet gives.

Talk about the line breaks in the poem.
Which lines rhyme?

 Write the words that rhyme in each line.

Words that Rhyme	

Why does the poet use rhyming words?
Share your answer.

_____

- -

_____

- -

_____

Talk about what senses are used to describe sitting in his Abuelita's lap.

Write the words that are used for each of the senses.

Tell	Hear	Listen To

How does the use of sense words help you know how the speaker feels? Share your answer.

_____

- -

_____

- -

 Write About It

Write a poem about a special person you know. Use repeating words. Share your answer.

Check In ⟩ 1 ⟩ 2 ⟩ 3 ⟩ 4 ⟩

Interview a Helper

Step 1 Pick a school helper to interview.

_____

- -

_____

Step 2 Decide what you want to know about
the school helper. Write your questions.

_____

- -

_____

_____

- -

_____

_____

- -

_____

Step 3 Interview the school helper.

Step 4 Write what you learned about the
school helper. Use a dictionary to find
and spell words to include in your writing.

_____

- -

_____

- -

_____

- -

_____

- -

_____

Step 5 Choose how to present your work.

Talk about the poem. How does the mother bird help little birdie?

 Compare the mother bird to the helpers in "All Kinds of Helpers."

Tennyson, Lord Alfred. "What Does Birdie Say?." In The Lullaby Book of Mother's Love Songs, compiled and arranged by Annie Blanche Shelby, 49. New York: Duffield & Company, 1921.

What Does Little Birdie Say?

What does little birdie say
In her nest at peep of day?
"Let me fly," says little birdie,
"Mother, let me fly away."
"Birdie, rest a little longer,
Till the little wings are stronger."
So she rests a little longer,
Then she flies away.

— Lord Alfred Tennyson

Quick Tip

You can talk about the mother bird using a sentence starter:

The mother bird tells the little birdie . . .

Check In 1 2 3 4

Write a Thank-You Letter

1 **Look** at your Build Knowledge pages in your reader's notebook. What did you learn about people who help others?

2 **Think** about a person who helps you.

3 **Write** a thank-you letter to this person. Then write about how this person is similar to or different from other people you read about who help. Use two vocabulary words from the Word Bank.

Think about what you learned this week. Fill in the bars on page 49.

Build Knowledge

Essential Question How can weather affect us?

Build Vocabulary

  Talk with your partner about different types of weather.

Write words about the weather.

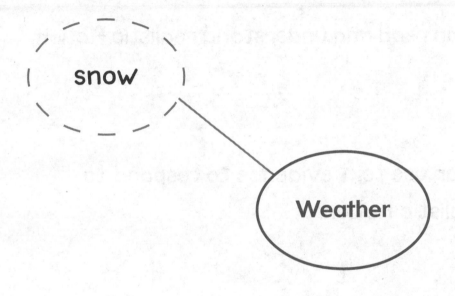

snow

Weather

My Goals

 Think about what you know now. We'll learn new things all week. Fill in the bars.

Key

1 =	I do not understand.
2 =	I understand but need more practice.
3 =	I understand.
4 =	I understand and can teach someone.

What I Know Now

I can read and understand realistic fiction.

1 > 2 > 3 > 4 >

I can use text evidence to respond to realistic fiction.

1 > 2 > 3 > 4 >

I know about how weather can affect us.

1 > 2 > 3 > 4 >

 You will come back to the next page later.

Think about what you've learned. Look back at your work. Fill in the bars.

What I Learned

I can read and understand realistic fiction.

> 1 > 2 > 3 > 4 >

I can use text evidence to respond to realistic fiction.

> 1 > 2 > 3 > 4 >

I know about how weather can affect us.

> 1 > 2 > 3 > 4 >

Shared Read

How can weather affect us?

My Goal I can read and understand realistic fiction.

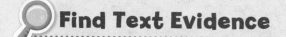 **Find Text Evidence**

Read to find out how icy weather affects a neighborhood.

 Circle and read aloud the word beginning with silent *w* as in *write*.

Wrapped in Ice

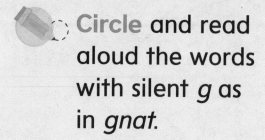 **Find Text Evidence**

Circle and read aloud the words with silent *g* as in *gnat*.

Think about the sound Kim hears. Talk about what you picture.

The sound of something hitting the window woke Kim up. *Ping! Ping, ping!* "What's that?" Kim asked herself.

Kim peeked outside. The trees were coated with ice. The yard sparkled. The driveway was like a skating rink. Even the car was wrapped in an icy design.

"Mom, why is everything covered in ice?" Kim wanted to know.

"That's a good question," said Mom. "Good thing I'm a science teacher! It's raining. But the air is very cold. So the raindrops freeze when they land on cold surfaces like signs, trees, and roads."

Shared Read

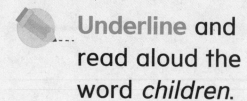

Underline and read aloud the word *children*.

Think about what the reporter says about the storm. Tell what you think the streets and roads look like.

Mom turned on the TV weather. A reporter said, "A winter storm has hit this part of the **country**. Freezing rain is making streets and roads icy. We advise you to stay inside! Children can stay home. Schools will be closed."

"We have a snow day!" cried Kim. "You mean an ice day!" laughed Mom.

Suddenly, all the lights went out!

"I guess some icy tree branches broke," said Mom. "They must have knocked down power lines. We won't have any power until the lines are fixed."

Kim looked worried. But Mom said, "Let's just pretend we are camping!"

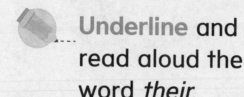 Underline and read aloud the word *their*.

Talk about what made everyone leave their houses.

Mom lit the logs in the fireplace. Kim got flashlights. They played lots of games. It was fun to eat their lunch by the fire.

Then Mom said, "Listen!" The *ping, ping, ping* had stopped!

"The storm must be over!" cried Kim.

Up and down the street, people came outside. There was so much to do. Everyone worked together. They put sand on the walks. They broke up the ice. Noses got red. Br-r-r-r! The air was very cold.

"I made a fire in the fireplace," Mom called out. "Come in and warm up!"

Retell the story using the words and illustrations to help you.

Neighbors came with flashlights and snacks. Ms. Knox brought cider. Mr. Wright told about the year it snowed in the month of May. Kim told knock-knock jokes.

"It's nice when everyone **gathers** together," said Mom.

Just then, the lights came on. Everyone cheered.

"It's been a big day!" smiled Mom. "We were lucky to be cozy and safe."

"We are lucky to have such nice neighbors, too," said Kim. "We turned an ice day into an ice party!"

Writing Practice

Write a Paragraph

 Talk about the weather from the story.

 Listen to this paragraph about weather.

> There was a big storm. The strong wind knocked down trees. The power went out! We stayed safe and warm inside until it was over.

 Underline the main idea.

 Circle any descriptive details.

Writing Traits

- The **main idea** tells what your writing is mostly about.

- **Descriptive details** give more information about your ideas.

Talk about a time weather affected you.

Write a paragraph about a time weather affected you. Make sure you include a main idea. Use descriptive details.

_____

_____

_____

_____

_____

_____

_____

Underline your main idea.

Circle any descriptive details you used.

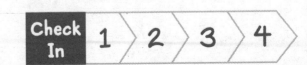

Vocabulary

  Listen to the sentences and look at the photos.

 Talk about the words.

Write your own sentence using each word.

country

This is a map of our **country**.

_____

- -

_____

gathers

She **gathers** some spring flowers.

_____

- -

_____

A simile can help you figure out what something is like. It uses the words *like* or *as* to compare one thing to another.

Find Text Evidence

I read this simile: "The driveway was like a skating rink." I know that skating rinks are made of ice and very slippery. The simile tells me the driveway was icy and slippery.

The driveway was like a skating rink.

Your Turn

Write what the simile in this sentence tells you: "It was like an oven outside."

_____

- - - - - - - - - - - - - - - - - - -

_____

- - - - - - - - - - - - - - - - - - -

_____

- - - - - - - - - - - - - - - - - - -

_____

Realistic fiction is a made-up story that could happen in real life. It can use dialogue, or words that characters say, to show what a character thinks and feels.

 Reread the story. Pay attention to the dialogue.

 Talk about the dialogue. What does it tell you about Kim and Mom?

 Write about the dialogue on page 89.

Check In 1 2 3 4

Dialogue	What the Dialogue Shows

In stories, one event causes another event to happen. Remember, a **cause** is the reason why something happens in a story. An **effect** is what happens.

 Reread "Wrapped in Ice."

 Talk about what the characters do and why they do it.

 Write about the causes and effects.

Check In 1 > 2 > 3 > 4 >

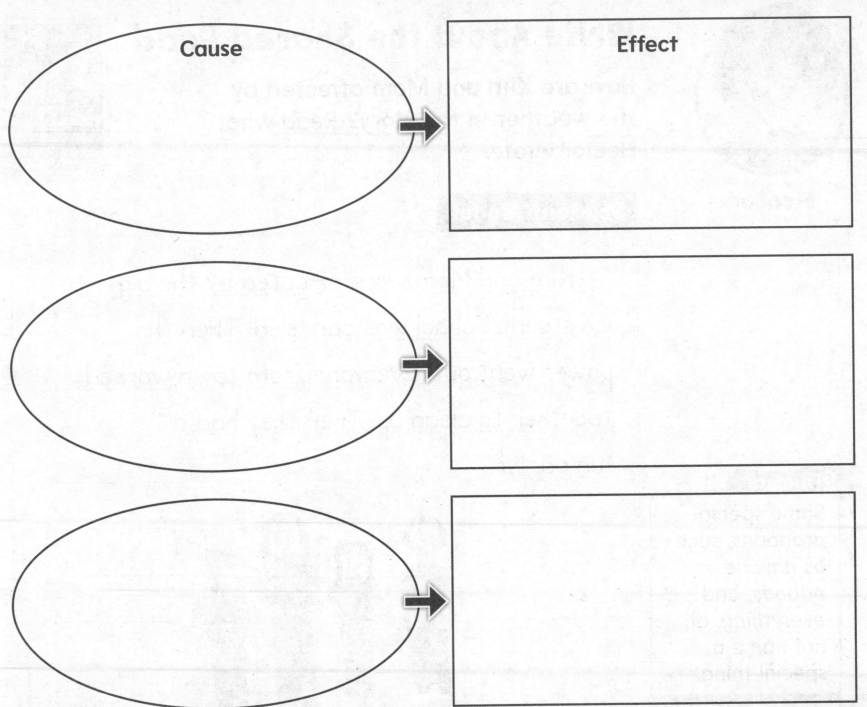

Cause

Effect

Writing and Grammar

Write About the Shared Read

How are Kim and Mom affected by the weather in the story? Read what Hector wrote.

Hector

Student Model

Kim and Mom were affected by the big ice storm. School was canceled. Then the power went out. Everyone from town worked together to clean up. Then they had a fun party!

BDLM/Cultura/Getty Images

Grammar

Some **special pronouns,** such as *anyone, nobody,* and *everything,* do not name a special thing.

Talk about details Hector used from the story. Underline the main idea.

Circle any special pronouns.

Draw boxes around descriptive details.

Write what you notice about Hector's writing.

Quick Tip

You can talk about Hector's writing using these sentence starters:

Hector used . . .
I noticed . . .

 Retell the story using the illustrations and words from the story.

Write about the story.

What does Thomas do to show that he's excited about the first day of school?

_____

_____

Text Evidence

Page

What is more important to the children than classrooms and desks?

_____

_____

Text Evidence

Page

Check In 1 2 3 4

Talk about what the school is like inside on pages 340–341.

 Write the words from the story that describe the school.

Words About the School

Why did the author include these words in the story? Share your answer.

_____

- -

_____

_____

- -

_____

 Talk about how the children feel on pages 346–349.

Write clues from the text and illustrations that let you know the children's feelings.

Text Clues	Illustration Clues

How does the author show how the children feel?
Share your answer.

_____

_____

_____

_____

Talk about what happens at the beginning and end of the story.

 Write about the school at the beginning and end of the story.

Beginning	End

Why is *Rain School* a good title for this book? Share your answer.

_____

_____

_____

_____

Check In 1 2 3 4

Write About the Anchor Text

What do the children in *Rain School* learn from their first lesson?

 Talk about the question.

 Write your answer below.

Rain School
by James Rumford

Remember:

☐ Include a main idea.

☐ Use descriptive details.

☐ Use special pronouns correctly.

Check In 1 2 3 4

Read to find out why we need rainy weather.

Underline the words that tell what the weather does.

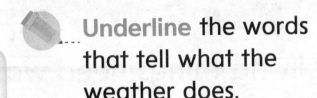

Talk about how you know the author will tell why rain is important.

Rainy Weather

Weather changes from day to day. Some days are sunny, and some days are rainy. When it rains, do you wish the rain would go away? You might, but we need rain.

Corbis/SuperStock

How Rain Helps

All living things need water. Rain helps plants grow, so that people and animals have food. Rain falls on ponds, lakes, and rivers. Then animals can drink water all year long. People need water to drink, too. We also use it for cooking and cleaning.

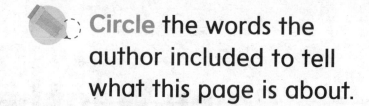

Circle the words the author included to tell what this page is about.

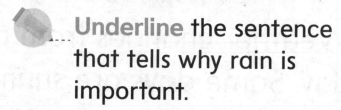

Underline the sentence that tells why rain is important.

Talk about why the author included the two photos on this page.

Quick Tip

Think about what the author tells about in the text.

Talk about what you learn in each section of the text.

 Write details from this section of the text.

How Rain Helps

How does the heading help organize the information? Share your answer.

_____

- -

_____

_____

- -

_____

Talk About It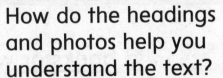

How do the headings and photos help you understand the text?

Check In 1 > 2 > 3 > 4

The Weather in My State

Step 1 **Decide** what you want to know about the weather in your state. Write your questions.

_____

_____

_____

_____

_____

Step 2 **Find** books or websites with the information you need. Read for answers to your questions.

Step 3 Write what you learned about your state's weather.

_____

- -

_____

- -

_____

- -

_____

_____

- -

_____

- -

_____

Step 4 Draw pictures to show the weather in your state.

Step 5 Choose how to present your work.

| Check In | 1 | 2 | 3 | 4 |

Talk about what you see happening in the painting. How is the sea affected?

 Compare the weather in the painting to the weather in *Rain School*.

Quick Tip

Describe what you see using this sentence starter:

The weather makes the sea . . .

This painting, *The Great Wave off Kanagawa* by Katsushika Hokusai, shows a huge wave next to boats.

Check In | 1 | 2 | 3 | 4

Create a Weather Safety Chart

1 **Look** at your Build Knowledge pages in your reader's notebook. What did you learn about ways weather can affect us?

2 **Create** a weather safety chart. Choose two types of weather you read about. Write how to stay safe in each type of weather. Use text evidence. Use two vocabulary words from the Word Bank.

3 **Draw** pictures for your weather safety chart.

Think about what you learned this week. Fill in the bars on page 85.

Build Knowledge

Build Vocabulary

 Talk with your partner about traditions you know.

 Write words about traditions.

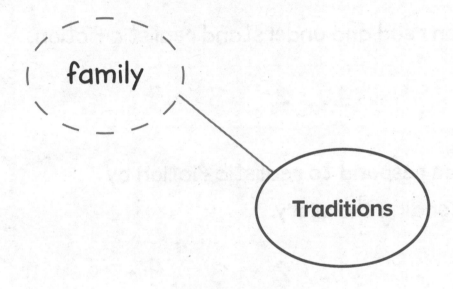

family

Traditions

My Goals

 Think about what you know now. Let's get going! Fill in the bars.

What I Know Now

I can read and understand realistic fiction.

1 > 2 > 3 > 4

I can respond to realistic fiction by extending the story.

1 > 2 > 3 > 4

I know about different types of traditions.

1 > 2 > 3 > 4

Key

1 = I do not understand.

2 = I understand but need more practice.

3 = I understand.

4 = I understand and can teach someone.

 You will come back to the next page later.

What I Learned

I can read and understand realistic fiction.

1 > 2 > 3 > 4

I can respond to realistic fiction by extending the story.

1 > 2 > 3 > 4

I know about different types of traditions.

1 > 2 > 3 > 4

My Goal I can read and understand realistic fiction.

🔍 **Find Text Evidence**

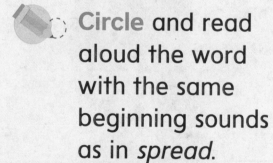 **Read** to find out how one family starts a new tradition.

Circle and read aloud the word with the same beginning sounds as in *spread*.

? What traditions do you know about?

A Spring Birthday

Talk about what Marco usually does for his birthday. How is it different from what he wants this year?

 Underline and read aloud the word *your*.

May was a happy time for Marco. It was his birthday month.

"Can I have a party this year?" he asked. "Then my friends can celebrate with me."

"It's our family tradition to have a birthday dinner," said Gram. "Your friends can join us. I will make *empanadas* for everyone."

"**Nobody** makes better *empanadas*, Gram!" Marco said. "But it would be fun to do something new this year."

Shared Read

 Find Text Evidence

 **Picture** and talk about what Marco's party will look like.

 Underline the words *heard*, *front*, and *push*.

"How about a picnic?" Dad asked. "I heard about a nice spot in the park on Elm Street. It's in front of the ball field. We can push the tables together."

"That sounds like fun," said Marco. "We can have hotdogs, burgers, and Gram's *empanadas!*"

At last, it was the morning of Marco's birthday. He opened his eyes. He saw Mom and Dad and Gram. They were singing the Mexican birthday song, "*Las mañanitas.*" Marco sprang out of bed. He could not wait for his party.

Find Text Evidence

 Talk about what the children do after lunch.

Circle and read aloud the word with the same beginning sounds as in *thrill*.

Mom and Dad went shopping before the party. First, they got a baseball mitt for Marco. Then they bought a birthday cake and a *piñata*.

Everyone met at the picnic spot. "Happy birthday! *Feliz cumpleaños, Marco!*" they shouted.

Mom hung the *piñata*. Dad spread out the food. There were hotdogs, burgers, and yummy *empanadas!*

After lunch, the children took turns striking the *piñata*. Each one swung three times. The *piñata* was **difficult** to hit! At last it split open. The kids shrieked and scrambled for the treats.

Shared Read

🔍 **Find Text Evidence**

 Retell the events of the story in order.

Next Marco opened his gifts. When he saw the baseball mitt, he cried, "Thank you! This is just what I wanted! I can use it in the game tomorrow."

When it was time for cake, Marco's family sang the Mexican birthday song again. Marco's friends hummed along. Then Mom taught them the words so they could sing it, too!

"This is the best birthday party I've ever had!" Marco said. "Can we do this again next year?"

"Sure," said Gram. "It's fun to mix the old with the new. A spring picnic can be your birthday tradition."

Write a Paragraph

 Talk about Marco's family's new tradition.

 Listen to this paragraph about a tradition.

A Spring Birthday

> Have you ever celebrated Arbor Day? It is my family's tradition to plant a tree on this day. We care for it all year. And we watch it grow!

 Talk about three different sentence types you notice.

 Talk about the beginning, middle, and end.

Writing Traits

- Use different sentence types like statements, questions, and exclamations.

- Include a **beginning, middle,** and **end** in your writing.

Talk about a tradition you have with your family.

Write a paragraph about a tradition you have with your family. Use different sentence types. Include a beginning, middle, and end.

_____

- -

_____

- -

_____

- -

_____

Talk about the different sentence types you used.

Talk about the beginning, middle, and end.

Vocabulary

 Listen to the sentences and look at the photos.

 Talk about the words.

 Write your own sentence using each word.

difficult

This puzzle is **difficult** to do.

_____

- -

_____

nobody

Nobody is on the porch.

_____

- -

_____

Alex Mares-Manton/Asia Images/Getty Images; David Papazian/Photographer's Choice RF/Getty Images

Compound Words

You can use the meaning of the smaller words in a compound word to figure out its meaning.

Find Text Evidence

I'm not sure what *birthday* means. The word is made up of two smaller words, *birth* and *day*. *Birth* refers to being born, so *birthday* is the day someone is born.

> May was a happy time for Marco. It was his birthday month.

Your Turn

What is the meaning of *everyone* on page 125?

_____

- - - - - - - - - - - - - - - - -

_____

- - - - - - - - - - - - - - - - -

_____

- - - - - - - - - - - - - - - - -

_____

_____

Check In 1 2 3 4

Remember, **realistic fiction** is a made-up story with characters, settings, and events that can happen in real life.

Reread to find out what makes this story realistic fiction.

Share how you know it is realistic fiction.

Write about the characters. Then write something they do that could happen in real life.

Check In 1 2 3 4

Who Could Be Real?	What Could Happen in Real Life?
1.	1.
2.	2.
3.	3.

The **theme** of a story is the message that the author wants to tell readers.

 Reread "A Spring Birthday."

 Talk about the clues in the story that help you understand the author's message.

 Write three clues that help you find the theme. Use the words and illustrations.

Check In | 1 | 2 | 3 | 4

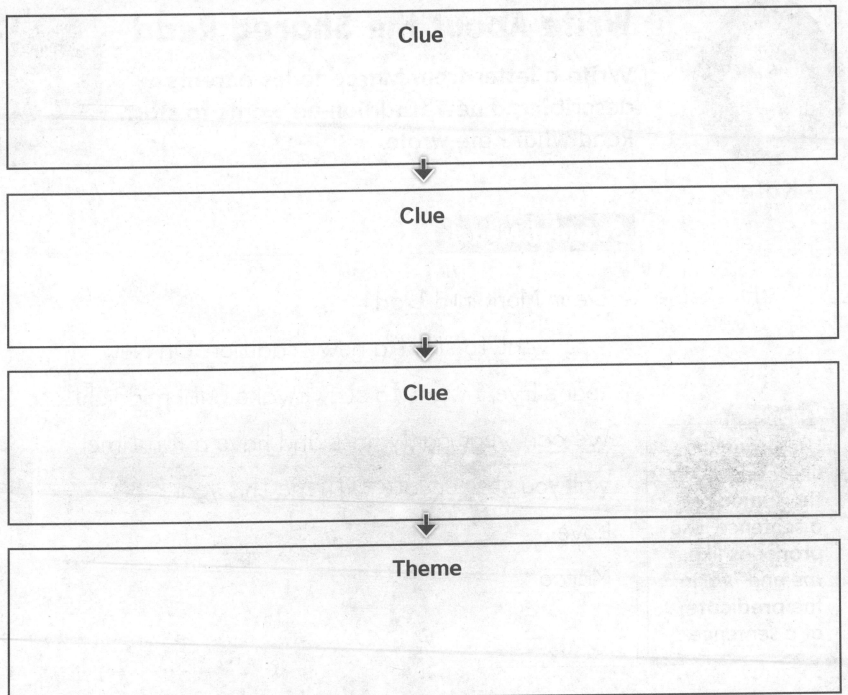

Clue

Clue

Clue

Theme

Kate

Write About the Shared Read

Write a letter from Marco to his parents describing a new tradition he wants to start. Read what Kate wrote.

strickke/iStock/Getty Images

Grammar

Use **pronouns** like *I* and *he* in the **subject** of a sentence. Use **pronouns** like *me* and *him* in the **predicate** of a sentence.

Student Model

Dear Mom and Dad,

    I want to start a new tradition. On New Year's Eve, I want to stay awake until midnight.

We can wear party hats and have a fun time!

Will you stay up late with me this year?

Love,

Marco

Talk about details Kate used. Draw a box around the question.

Circle the subject pronoun in the first sentence. Circle the object pronoun in the last sentence.

Underline the beginning blue. Underline the middle orange. Underline the ending green.

Write what you notice about Kate's writing.

Quick Tip

You can talk about Kate's writing using these sentence starters:

Kate used . . .
I noticed . . .

Retell the story using the illustrations and words from the story.

Write about the story.

Why does Lissy make Menu?

_____

- -

_____

- -

_____

Text Evidence

Page

How does Lissy make her first real friend?

_____

- -

_____

- -

_____

Text Evidence

Page

Check In | 1 | 2 | 3 | 4

Talk about what happens in the text and illustrations on pages 374–377.

Write clues about how Lissy feels.

Text	Illustrations

Lissy feels ...

How does the author show you how Lissy feels? Share your answer.

_____

_____

_____

 Talk about what happens outside Lissy's window on pages 378–379.

Write clues from the text and illustration.

Text	Illustration

Lissy sees ...

How does the author show how Lissy feels when she looks outside? Share your answer.

_____

_____

_____

Talk about what is happening on pages 388–389.

 Write clues that show how things are different for Lissy now.

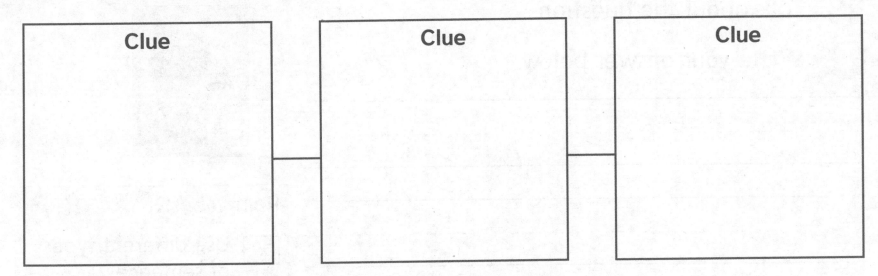

Clue	Clue	Clue

How do you know that things are different now? Share your answer.

_____

- -

_____

- -

_____

Check In 1 2 3 4

Writing and Grammar

Write About the Anchor Text

Write a letter from Lissy to her paper friends telling them how things are going now.

 Talk about the question.

 Write your answer below.

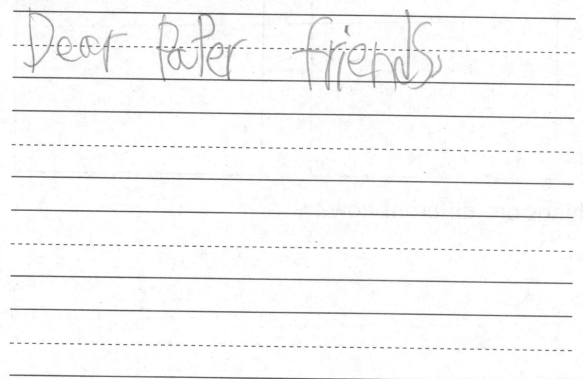

Dear Paper friends,

Remember:

- [ ] Use different types of sentences.

- [ ] Include a beginning, middle, and end.

- [ ] Use subject and object pronouns correctly.

Check In 1 2 3 4

Making Paper Shapes

See the crane made out of folded paper? Folding paper to make different shapes is called origami. People in Asia have made origami for hundreds of years.

Kids learn this art from their mothers, fathers, and grandparents.

Read to learn about origami.

Circle the words that tell what the crane is made of.

Talk about why the author included the photo on this page.

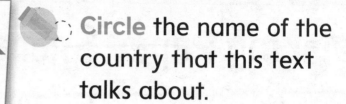

People in Japan make decorations for special days. One holiday is the Star Festival. Children sing songs and get treats to eat.

Families hang bright origami in the streets. Kids write wishes on slips of paper and hang them from sticks. They hope their wishes come true.

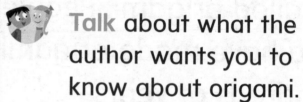

Circle the name of the country that this text talks about.

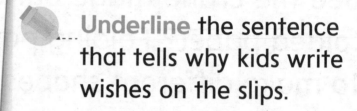

Underline the sentence that tells why kids write wishes on the slips.

Talk about what the author wants you to know about origami.

Quick Tip

You can use this sentence starter:

The author shows readers …

Meg Takamura/Age fotostock

Talk about the information on each page.

Write what the information on each page is about.

page 147	
page 148	

Why does the author organize the text this way?
Share your answer.

_____

- -

_____

- -

_____

Talk About It

What other photo would make sense on page 148? What would it show?

Check In 1 2 3 4

Interview About Traditions

Step 1 **Pick** a partner to interview about a family tradition they have or know about.

_____

- -

_____

Step 2 **Decide** what questions you want to ask.

_____

- -

_____

_____

- -

_____

_____

- -

_____

Step 3 **Ask** your questions.

Step 4 Write the answers to your questions.

_____

- - - - - - - - - - - - - - - - - - -

_____

- - - - - - - - - - - - - - - - - - -

_____

- - - - - - - - - - - - - - - - - - -

_____

- - - - - - - - - - - - - - - - - - -

_____

- - - - - - - - - - - - - - - - - - -

_____

- - - - - - - - - - - - - - - - - - -

_____

Step 5 Draw something from your partner's tradition.

Step 6 Choose how to present your work.

Check In 1 2 3 4

Talk about the photo. How are the girls sharing a tradition?

 Compare how the girls' tradition is similar to and different from the traditions in "A Spring Birthday."

These girls perform Irish step dancing like their mothers and grandmothers did.

felix zaska/Alamy Stock Photo

Quick Tip

You can compare both traditions using these sentence starters:

The girls' tradition . . .

The traditions in "A Spring Birthday" . . .

Check In 1 > 2 > 3 > 4 >

Create a Classroom Book

1 Look at your Build Knowledge pages in your reader's notebook. What did you learn about traditions?

2 Write about a tradition in your family. Write how it is similar to or different from the traditions you read about. Use text evidence. Use two vocabulary words from the Word Bank.

3 Draw your family tradition. Tell a partner what makes it a good tradition.

Think about what you learned this week. Fill in the bars on page 121.

Build Knowledge

? Essential Question **Why do we celebrate holidays?**

Build Vocabulary

 Talk with your partner about ways people celebrate.

 Write words about celebrations.

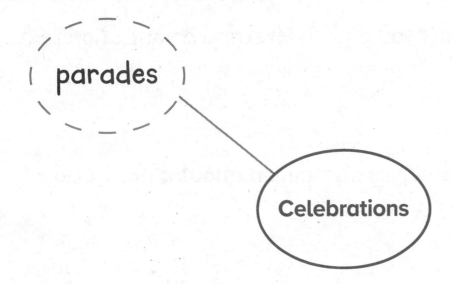

parades

Celebrations

My Goals

 Think about what you know now. What do you need to practice more? Fill in the bars.

What I Know Now

I can read and understand a nonfiction text.

1 > 2 > 3 > 4

I can write my opinion about a nonfiction text.

1 > 2 > 3 > 4

I know about why we celebrate holidays.

1 > 2 > 3 > 4

Key
1 = I do not understand.
2 = I understand but need more practice.
3 = I understand.
4 = I understand and can teach someone.

 You will come back to the next page later.

Think about what you've learned. How did you do? Fill in the bars.

What I Learned

I can read and understand a nonfiction text.

1 > 2 > 3 > 4

I can write my opinion about a nonfiction text.

1 > 2 > 3 > 4

I know about why we celebrate holidays.

1 > 2 > 3 > 4

Shared Read

My Goal
I can read and understand a nonfiction text.

Find Text Evidence

Read to find out how people celebrate the harvest.

Circle and read aloud the word spelled with *are* as in *care*.

Essential Question

? Why do we celebrate holidays?

PierreDesrosiers/iStock/Getty Images

Share the Harvest and Give Thanks

Circle and read aloud the word spelled with *air* as in *hair.*

 Reread and use what you know to be sure you understand what "celebrate the harvest" means.

Say Thanks

In our **nation**, families celebrate the harvest in a number of ways. You can eat a harvest dinner at home, or you can go to a fair or festival. Harvest is a time to **unite** with friends and family. It is also a time when people share harvest foods.

Farm stands have harvest fruits and vegetables. These may include pumpkins and apples in the fall and berries and tomatoes in the spring.

All across the United States, people give thanks for the fall harvest. This day is called Thanksgiving. It is on the fourth Thursday in November. Families eat together and show that they are thankful.

Isadora Getty Buyou/Photodisc/Getty Images

Shared Read

Find Text Evidence

 Underline and read aloud the words *favorite* and *gone*.

 Reread and use the photos to be sure you understand Thanksgiving and Kwanzaa.

Many families eat a special meal on Thanksgiving. Foods that are harvested in the fall may be part of the celebration.

The first Thanksgiving in our nation was in 1621. Today, families and friends still give thanks with a feast. They may eat such favorite foods as turkey, corn, and green beans. People like to enjoy the harvest foods before they are gone.

Radius Images/Corbis

Kwanzaa is also a family celebration. It is based on the harvest. Corn and fruit are symbols of the holiday. Families celebrate with a feast.

Kwanzaa begins on December 26. It celebrates the harvest of Africa. Many people in the United States celebrate Kwanzaa.

Mark Adams/The Image Bank/Getty Images

Shared Read

🔍 **Find Text Evidence**

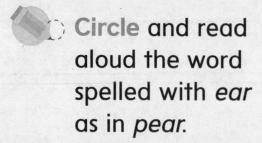

Circle and read aloud the word spelled with *ear* as in *pear*.

Underline and read aloud the words *young, few,* and *surprise*.

Harvest Festivals

In many states, Thanksgiving is a fun affair! Some places hold big parades where people march, sing, and dance. At one parade, young actors wear costumes. They act out the first Thanksgiving. That is so you can see what harvest was like so many years ago.

In Plymouth, the city of the first Thanksgiving, some people dress up like Pilgrims.

First Thanksgiving 1621
Plimoth, Massachusetts

At the Kentucky Harvest Festival, the corn crop is the star. Kids have a contest to peel the most ears of corn. Families join teams to play a Cornhole Toss game. The teams toss a few bags filled with corn kernels. They follow rules to score. The winning team gets a surprise!

A bean-bag toss game is popular at Kentucky and Ohio harvest festivals. Players pitch their corn bags and try to get them into a hole.

Shared Read

🔍 **Find Text Evidence**

Retell the text using the photos and words to help you.

In some places, pumpkins are a BIG deal! Large pumpkins are dug out and used as boats. After the race the pumpkins are used for compost, or to make new dirt.

Row, row, row your pumpkin! These giant pumpkins make a splash at Oregon's Giant Pumpkin Race.

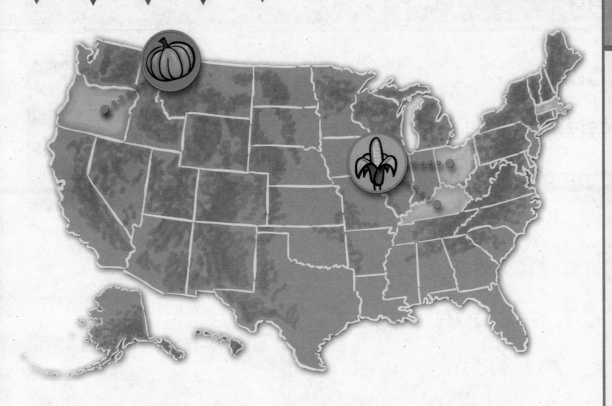

Key

 Pumpkin Race in Oregon

Corn Festivals in
Kentucky and Ohio

Across the nation, people celebrate the harvest. At home or with others, it is no wonder that harvest is a fun time for all!

Write a Paragraph

Talk about ways to celebrate the harvest.

Listen to this paragraph about a holiday.

> My favorite holiday is Earth Day. At school, we plant flowers. At home, we volunteer to clean in town. We help Earth on this day!

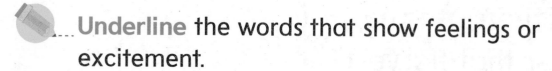 **Underline** the words that show feelings or excitement.

 **Circle** the reasons for the opinion.

Writing Traits

- Authors can use words that show feelings or excitement.

- Remember, always include **reasons for your opinion**.

Talk about your favorite holiday to celebrate.

Write a paragraph about your favorite holiday. Use words that show your feelings. Include reasons for your opinion.

_____

_____

_____

_____

_____

_____

Underline the words that show your feelings or excitement.

Circle the reasons for your opinion.

Check In 1 2 3 4

Vocabulary

 Listen to the sentences and look at the photos.

 Talk about the words.

 Write your own sentence using each word.

nation

Our **nation** has 50 states.

_____

- - - - - - - - - - - - - - - - - -

_____

unite

We all **unite** to help the Earth.

_____

- - - - - - - - - - - - - - - - - -

_____

A metaphor compares one thing to another.
It helps you picture what the thing is like.

Find Text Evidence

The metaphor "the corn crop is the star"
compares corn with a star. I know a star can
be a popular person who people like. This tells
me the corn is popular with people.

> At the Kentucky Harvest Festival,
> the (corn crop) is the (star.)

Your Turn

What does the metaphor "Ron is a giant"
tell you about Ron?

_____

_____

Check In 1 2 3 4

Shared Read

A **nonfiction** text tells about real people, places, things, and events. It can tell why something happens.

 Reread to find out what makes this text nonfiction.

 Talk about how and why people celebrate the harvest on pages 160–163.

 Write how and why people celebrate the harvest.

Check In 1 2 3 4

How People Celebrate the Harvest	Why People Celebrate the Harvest
	there is Lot of food food

Remember, the **author's purpose** is the reason why an author writes a text. The author can use information in the text and photos to explain his or her purpose.

 Reread "Share the Harvest and Give Thanks."

 Talk about what information you learn from the photos.

 Write about the different information you get from the text and photos. Write how they tell you the author's purpose.

Check In | 1 > 2 > 3 > 4 >

Clues

Clues

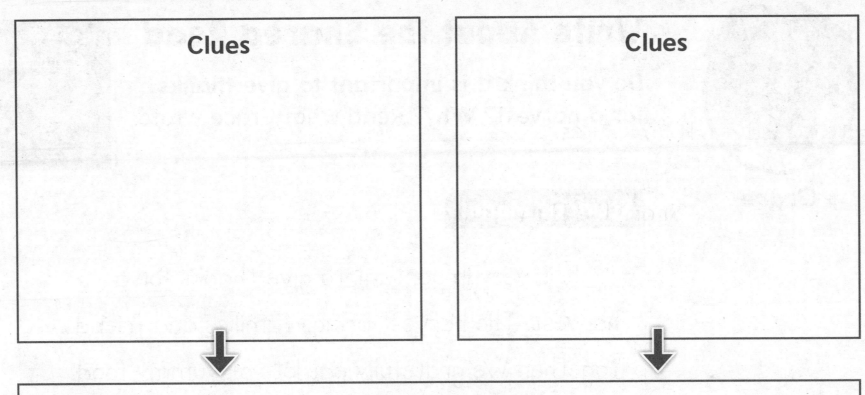

Author's Purpose

Grace

Write About the Shared Read

Do you think it is important to give thanks for a harvest? Why? Read what Grace wrote.

Student Model

It is very important to give thanks for a harvest. The harvest brings families and friends together. We gratefully eat lots of yummy food. I feel lucky to celebrate the harvest. We can all give thanks together!

Grammar

An **adverb** tells more about a verb. Some adverbs **tell how** an action happened.

Talk about details Grace used from the text. Underline words that tell how Grace feels.

Circle an adverb that tells how.

Draw a box around Grace's reasons for her opinion.

Write what you notice about Grace's writing.

Quick Tip

You can talk about Grace's writing using these sentence starters:

Grace used . . .
I noticed . . .

 Retell the text using the photos and words from the text.

Write about the text.

Why did the colonies want to split away from England?

_____

_____

_____

Text Evidence

Page

How did the people of the colonies let the king know what they wanted?

_____

_____

_____

Text Evidence

Page

Check In 1 > 2 > 3 > 4 >

Talk about the information the author gives on pages 399–401.

 Write about the information *before* the question at the end of page 399. Write about the information *after* the question.

Before	After

How does the author organize the information in the text?

_____

- -

_____

_____

- -

_____

 Talk about how the author uses dates on pages 402–403.

 Write what happened on the dates. Use clues from the text.

On July 4, 1776		On July 4 one year later

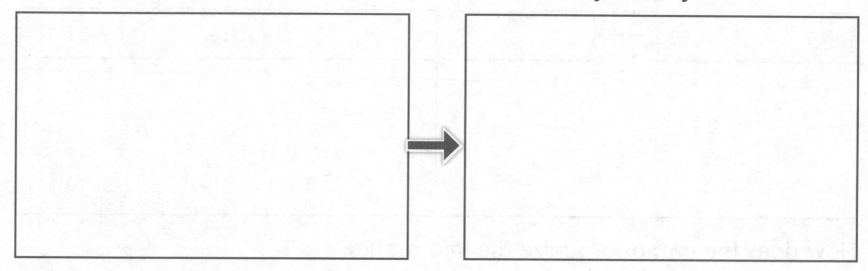

Why does the author use dates in the text?
Share your answer.

_____

_____

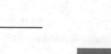 Check In 1 2 3 4

Writing and Grammar

Write About the Anchor Text

My Goal I can write my opinion about a nonfiction text.

Which part of the Fourth of July celebration is most important to you? Use text evidence.

 Talk about the question.

Write your answer below.

_____

- -

_____

_____

_____

- -

_____

_____

- -

_____

Remember:

☐ Include words that tell how you feel.

☐ Include reasons for your opinion.

☐ Use adverbs that tell how correctly.

Check In 1 2 3 4

Martin Luther King, Jr. Day

Every year, Americans celebrate Dr. Martin Luther King, Jr.'s birthday. Dr. King was a civil rights hero.

Many states hold parades. People give speeches. There is a national day of service. On this day, we can help others. We can deliver meals, clean up parks, and paint homes.

A girl makes sandwiches for others.

 Read to find out about how Americans celebrate Dr. Martin Luther King, Jr.'s birthday.

 Underline the ways people celebrate this holiday.

 Talk about why the author chose this photo for the text.

The Washington Post/Getty Images

Talk about the photo and caption.

 Compare the information you get from the text, photo, and caption.

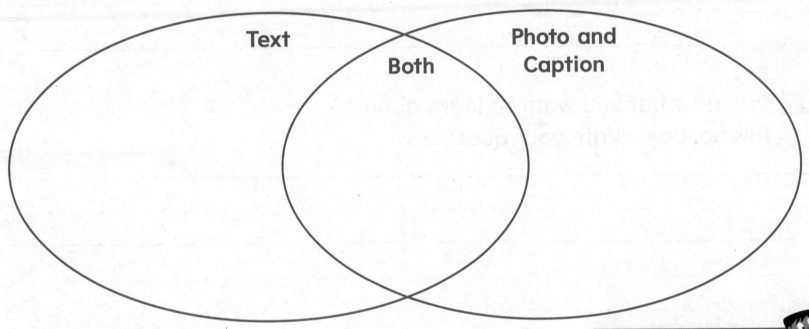

Text

Both

Photo and Caption

How do the photo and caption help you understand the text?

_____

- -

_____

Talk About It

What are some ways you would like to celebrate Dr. King's birthday?

| Check In | 1 | 2 | 3 | 4 |

Research and Inquiry

Find Out About a Holiday

Step 1 **Pick** a holiday to research.

_____

- -

_____

Step 2 **Decide** what you want to learn about this holiday. Write your questions.

_____

- -

_____

- -

_____

- -

_____

Step 3 **Find** the information you need in books or online. Read for answers to your questions.

Step 4 **Write** what you learned about your holiday. Use a dictionary to find and spell words about the holiday.

_____

- -

_____

- -

_____

- -

_____

- -

_____

- -

_____

Step 5 **Draw** a way that people celebrate this holiday.

Step 6 **Choose** how to present your work.

| Check In | 1 | 2 | 3 | 4 |

Sing the song. Talk about what makes America special in the song.

 Compare this song to the holidays in "Share the Harvest and Give Thanks."

Quick Tip

Describe the song using these sentence starters:

The song is about . . .

It says America is . . .

from You're a Grand Old Flag

You're a grand old flag,
    you're a high-flying flag;

And forever in peace
    may you wave;

You're the emblem of
    the land I love;

The home of the free
    and the brave.

— George M. Cohan

Check In 1 2 3 4

Write About a Holiday

1 **Look** at your Build Knowledge pages in your reader's notebook. What did you learn about ways we celebrate holidays?

2 **Write** about your favorite holiday and how you celebrate it.

3 **Write** about how your celebration is similar to or different from the ones you read about. Use two vocabulary words from the Word Bank.

Think about what you learned this week. Fill in the bars on page 157.

Writing and Grammar

Gia

I wrote an opinion text. I included reasons for my opinion.

Opinion

My text tells how I feel and gives my reasons why.

Student Model

Which Helper?

There are lots of helper jobs, like doctors, teachers, and bus drivers. Which helper job would I like most?

I would like to be a sports coach. In "All Kinds of Helpers," I read that baseball coaches teach their teams how to hold the ball. Coaches teach them the rules of baseball.

My soccer coach shows us how to score a goal. She teaches us how to kick. She helps us a lot! I like helping people, so I think I would be a good coach.

I think coaches are important helpers for kids. A coach is the job for me!

 Talk about what makes Gia's writing an opinion.

 Ask any questions you have.

 Underline the sentences that tell Gia's opinion.

Writing and Grammar

Brainstorm and Plan

 Talk about helpers you read about.

 Draw or **write** about helper jobs that you might like to have.

Quick Tip

You can use these sentence starters:

I would like to be . . .

It is a good job because . . .

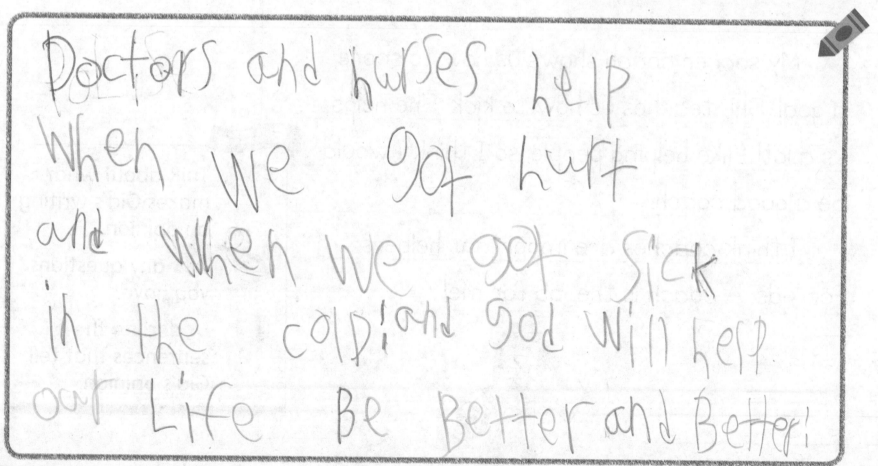

Doctors and nurses help when we got hurt and when we got sick in the cold and God will help our Life Be Better and Better!

Choose one helper to write about.

I Choose Life god.

List two reasons for your opinion. Include one from the text.

Draft

Read Gia's draft of her opinion.

> **Student Model**
>
> ### Which Helper?
>
> There are lots of helper jobs, like doctors, teachers, and bus drivers. Which helper job would I like most?
>
> I would like to be a sports coach. In "All Kinds of Helpers," I read that baseball coaches teach their teams how to hold the ball.

Reasons Based on a Source

I included reasons based on a book I read.

Voice

I showed my feelings and excitement.

My soccer coach shows us how to score a goal. She teaches us how to kick. She helps us a lot! I like helping people, so I think I would be a good coach.

I think coaches are important helpers for kids.

Sentence Types

I used different sentence types to make my writing more interesting.

Your Turn

Begin to write your opinion text in your writer's notebook. Use your ideas from pages 190–191. Include important facts and words that show your feelings.

Check In 1 2 3 4

Writing and Grammar

Revise and Edit

Think about how Gia revised and edited her opinion text.

Student Model

Which Helper?

There are lots of helper jobs, like doctors, teachers, and bus drivers. Which helper job would I like most?

I would like to be a sports coach. In "All Kinds of Helpers," I read that baseball coaches teach their teams how to hold the ball. Coaches teach them the rules of baseball.

I used capital letters at the beginning of sentences and for the pronoun *I*.

I added another reason to be more convincing.

Grammar

- Pronouns are words that can take the place of nouns. They can be subjects or objects.

- Possessive pronouns tell who or what owns or has something.

I made sure to use the possessive pronoun *My* correctly.

My soccer coach shows us how to score a goal. She teaches us how to kick. She helps us a lot! I like helping people, so I think I would be a good coach.

I think coaches are important helpers for kids. A coach is the job for me!

Concluding Statement

I added more information to make my ending more interesting.

Your Turn

Revise and edit your writing in your writer's notebook. Be sure to include a concluding statement.

Check In 1 2 3 4

Publish and Present

 Finish editing your writing. Make sure it is neat and ready to publish.

 Practice presenting your work with a partner. Use this checklist.

 Present your work.

Review Your Work	Yes	No
Speaking and Listening		
I used the correct tone for my writing.	☐	☐
I spoke loudly and clearly.	☐	☐
I listened carefully.	☐	☐
I used complete sentences.	☐	☐

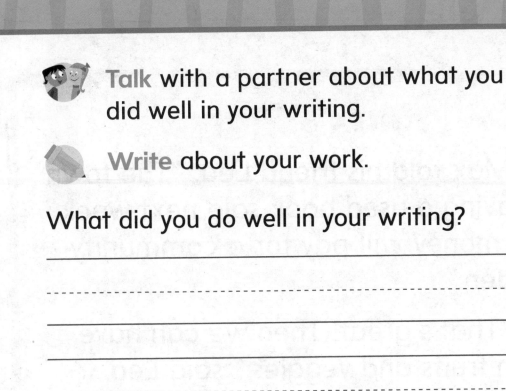

Talk with a partner about what you did well in your writing.

Write about your work.

What did you do well in your writing?

_____

- -

_____

_____

- -

_____

What do you need to work on?

_____

- -

_____

_____

- -

_____

 Think about your goal of writing an opinion text. Fill in the bars.

Check In | 1 > 2 > 3 > 4 >

Together We Can! **197**

My Goal I can read and understand social studies texts.

Find Text Evidence

Ask yourself questions about the text. Read to find the answers.

Circle the words that tell Max's plan.

Talk about how a garden will help Max's community.

Max's Plan

Max told his friend Lea, "The town is having a used book sale next week. The money will pay for a community garden."

"That's great! Then we can have fresh fruits and veggies," said Lea.

"My mom says a garden helps improve the environment, too," said Max. "Let's make flyers!"

"Good plan!" said Lea.

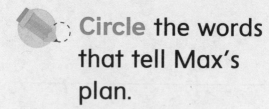

Take Notes

Max and his friends made a lot of flyers. Then they handed them all out. "I hope that works," said Max.

Max and his mom drove to the sale. "Why aren't we moving?" he asked.

"There is too much traffic," said his mom.

As they finally got closer, Max saw why. "Look at the crowds," he shouted. "Our flyers worked!" And the town was able to get a community garden!

Connect to Social Studies

Ask yourself questions about the text. Read to find the answers.

Circle ways we can recycle.

Talk about why it is important to recycle. Use details from the text.

Let's Recycle!

People make a lot of trash. Most people throw away more than 1,000 pounds of trash each year. Much of that trash ends up in our seas or in big pits in the ground. That's why it is important to recycle!

One way to recycle is to reuse things. You can trade old toys with a friend instead of buying new ones. You can make a fun swing from a boring old car tire.

Recycling also takes old things and makes new things. Plastic milk jugs can be recycled to make playground slides. Water bottles can be recycled to make tee-shirts.

How can you help? Don't throw away paper, cardboard, cans, plastic, or glass. You can put it all in special recycling bins. That will help make much less trash. And less trash means a cleaner planet.

Take Notes

Compare the Passages

 Talk about how "Max's Plan" and "Let's Recycle!" are the same and different.

 Compare and contrast the ways people can help their communities in each text.

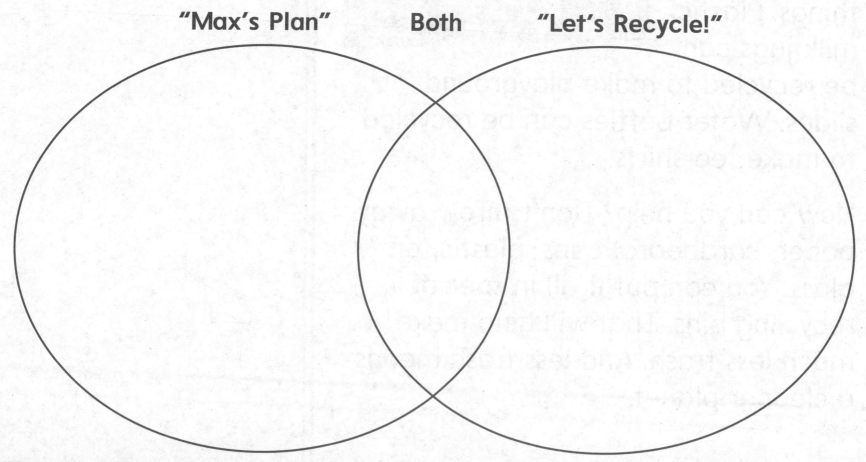

"Max's Plan"   Both   "Let's Recycle!"

Write the ways people can help their communities in each text.

_____

- -

_____

- -

_____

- -

_____

- -

_____

- -

_____

Take Action Poster

 Talk about different ways you can help your community.

What to do

1. Make a plan to help your community.

2. Draw a poster to share your plan with others.

3. Add details to your drawing.

4. Write a title for your poster.

5. Share your plan with a partner.

You need

pencil

crayons

Choose Your Own Book

Minutes I Read

 Tell a partner about a book you want to read. Say why you want to read it.

✏️ **Write** the title.

_____

- - - - - - - - - - - - - - - - - -

_____

✏️ **Write** your opinion of the book. Give reasons to support your opinion.

_____

- - - - - - - - - - - - - - - - - -

_____

_____

- - - - - - - - - - - - - - - - - -

_____

Think About Your Learning

Think about what you learned this unit.

Write one thing you did well.

_____

- - - - - - - - - - - - - - - - - - -

_____

_____

- - - - - - - - - - - - - - - - - - -

_____

Write one thing that you want to get better at.

_____

- - - - - - - - - - - - - - - - - - -

_____

_____

- - - - - - - - - - - - - - - - - - -

Share a goal you have with a partner.

My Sound-Spellings

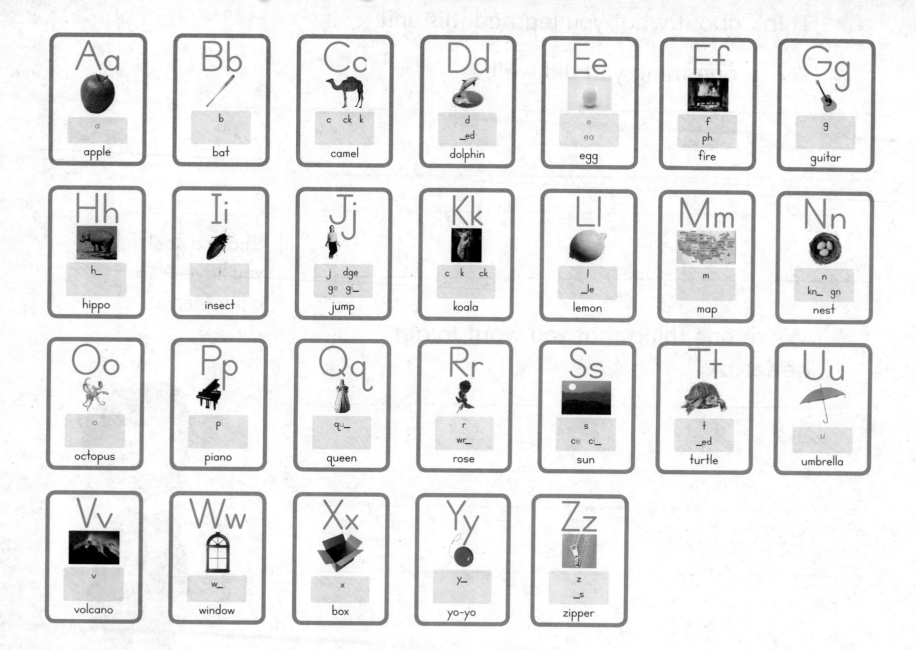

Aa a apple	**Bb** b bat	**Cc** c ck k camel	**Dd** d _ed dolphin	**Ee** e ea egg	**Ff** f ph fire	**Gg** g guitar
Hh h_ hippo	**Ii** i insect	**Jj** j dge ge gi_ jump	**Kk** c k ck koala	**Ll** l _le lemon	**Mm** m map	**Nn** n kn_ gn nest
Oo o octopus	**Pp** p piano	**Qq** qu_ queen	**Rr** r wr_ rose	**Ss** s ce ci_ sun	**Tt** t _ed turtle	**Uu** u umbrella
Vv v volcano	**Ww** w_ window	**Xx** x box	**Yy** y_ yo-yo	**Zz** z _s zipper		

Credits: (apple) Stockdisc/PunchStock; (bat) Radlund & Associates/Artville/Getty Images; (camel) Photodisc/Getty Images; (dolphin) imagebroker/Alamy; (egg) Pixtal/age fotostock; (fire) Comstock Images/Alamy; (guitar) Jules Frazier/Getty Images; (hippo) Michele Burgess/Corbis; (insect) Photodisc/Getty Images; (jump) Rubberball Productions/Getty Images; (koala) Al Franklin/Corbis; (lemon) C Squared Studios/Getty Images; (map) McGraw-Hill Education; (nest) Siede Preis/Photodisc/Getty Images; (octopus) Photographers Choice RF/SuperStock; (piano) Photo Spin/Getty Images; (queen) Joshua Ets-Hokin/Photodisc/Getty Images; (rose) Steve Cole/Photodisc/Getty Images; (sun) 97/E+/Getty Images; (turtle) Ingram Publishing/Fotosearch; (umbrella) Stockbyte/PunchStock; (volcano) Westend6l/Getty Images; (window) Photodisc/Getty Images; (box) C Squared Studios/Getty Images; (yo-yo) D. Hurst/Alamy; (zipper) ImageState/Alamy

th

thumb

sh

shell

ch
tch

cheese

wh_

whale

ng

sing

a ai_ _ay
a_e ea ei

train

i y i_e
igh ie

five

o oa ow
o_e _oe

boat

u u_e
_ew _ue

cube

e_e ea ee
e _y
ie _ey

tree

ar

star

er ir
ur or

shirt

oar or ore

corn

ow
ou

cow

oi
_oy

boy

oo

book

oo u_e u
_ew ue
ou ui

spoon

a aw au
augh al

straw

air are
ear ere

chair

Aa Bb Cc Dd Ee

Ff Gg Hh Ii Jj

Kk Ll Mm Nn

Oo Pp Qq Rr

Ss Tt Uu Vv

Ww Xx Yy Zz